SERMON OUTLINES
FOR
Invitations to Christ

GENE WILLIAMS

Beacon Hill Press of Kansas City
Kansas City, Missouri

Unless otherwise indicated all Scripture quotations are taken from the *Holy Bible, New International Version*® (NIV®). Copyright © 1973, 1978, 1984 by International Bible Society. Used by permission of Zondervan Publishing House. All rights reserved.

Scripture from the *Amplified New Testament* (AMP.), copyright © 1954, 1958, 1987 by The Lockman Foundation. Used by permission.

Scripture from the *Holy Bible, New Living Translation* (NLT), copyright © 1996. Used by permission of Tyndale House Publishers, Inc., Wheaton, IL 60189. All rights reserved.

Scripture from *The New Testament in Modern English* (PHILLIPS), Revised Student Edition, by J. B. Phillips, translator, reprinted with the permission of the Macmillan Publishing Company. Copyright 1958, 1960, 1972 by J. B. Phillips.

Library of Congress Cataloging-in-Publication Data

Williams, Gene, 1932-
    Sermon outlines for invitations to Christ / Gene Williams.
        p. cm. — (Beacon sermon outline series)
    ISBN 0-8341-2062-3 (pbk.)
    1. Evangelistic sermons—Outlines, syllabi, etc. 2. Bible—Sermons—Outlines, syllabi, etc.
I. Title. II. Series.

    BV3797.W47 2003
    251'.3—dc21

                                                                    2003009637

10   9   8   7   6   5   4   3   2   1

Contents

Introduction

We live in a day when people need to be confronted about their relationship with Jesus Christ. The messages in this volume are prepared with that in mind. It should be noted that every message we preach will in some way impact the relationship of the listeners to our Savior.

These messages offer a broad base of appeals for spiritual action. Some of them speak to church members who have become careless about their spiritual lives. Others will expose sinful living for the destructive path that it is. Still other messages will point out the critical necessity of making a decision to bring our spiritual lives into a proper relationship with Jesus.

In every situation the bottom line is the question Pilate asked in Matt. 27:22, "What shall I do . . . with Jesus who is called Christ?" The time is upon us to confront our world with that question.

These are strong messages calling for critical decisions. Preach them from a full heart and in the same spirit Jesus displayed when He confronted the rich young man in Matt. 19:16.

It is critical to remember that people cannot be driven to Jesus. Simply present the truth of scripture from a heart warmed by the fires of His holy altar. In doing so you will lift up Jesus who said in John 12:32, "But I, when I am lifted up from the earth, will draw all men to myself."

Sin and the Savior

1 Timothy 1:15

Introduction

A. We can never fully appreciate Jesus until we understand the seriousness of sin. We need to have a healthy awareness of sin and its consequences.

B. Paul had a keen awareness of sin. He remembered the years of unbelief and persecution of Christians. He sensed his own need and dependence upon Jesus as Savior. He responded to this in our text. Read 1 Tim. 1:15.

C. If we are to make it to heaven and enjoy an eternity with our Lord, we must also have this awareness of sin and the Savior.

I. We Need a Conviction of the Reality of Sin

A. The scripture makes it clear that sin is no optical illusion or mirage. In Rom. 3:23 we read, "All have sinned and fall short of the glory of God." In Rom. 5:12 we read, "Death came to all men, because all sinned." Multiple scriptures teach the realities of sin.

B. Everyone must admit, "I have sinned," regardless of his or her definition of sin.

C. Sin has been defined in many ways. It is defined as overstepping the line between right and wrong. Sin can be described as missing the mark or failure to meet the divine standard. It can be called lawlessness—spiritual anarchy. It can be defined as trespass—the intrustion of self-will into the divine authority. Sin is a willful transgression that violates God's laws.

D. Whatever definition is used, sin is so real that God could not ignore it.

II. We Need a Conviction of the Ruined Lives That Come from Sin

A. Some people try to make light of sin. Sin is part of our

animal nature that has not been conquered. Sin is a backwash in our upward climb to perfection.

B. We must understand that sin is destructive to body and soul.

    1. Sin is not something to be taken lightly. Sin is deadly (Rom. 6:23). Sin is like a bomb that is ready to explode and ruin sinners' lives.

    2. God has not revoked the sentence on sinful living. "Sin, when it is full-grown, gives birth to death" (James 1:15).

III. The Gospel of Jesus Offers the Remedy for Sin (see text)

A. The Bible does not minimize sin. It reveals sin for what it is but magnifies grace. Paul addressed this in Rom. 5:20-21 and in 6:14.

B. Sin is:

    1. A debt that Jesus Christ paid for us in full (John 3:16).

    2. A cloud that Jesus dispelled to show us the face of our Father.

    3. A burden from which Christ sets us free (John 8:36).

    4. A stain that Jesus Christ washes away (Isa. 1:18).

    5. Death—but Jesus offers life (Rom. 6:23).

C. God's grace is more than sufficient for all sin but is limited to our freewill.

Conclusion

A. Sin is real—it is destructive and brings eternal condemnation. It has created destruction since the beginning. Illustrate with what happened in the Garden of Eden with Adam and Eve.

B. The good news is that Jesus Christ came to save sinners. As powerful as the grip of sin was on Paul before he met Christ, the grace provided by Jesus was more powerful.

C. Jesus will change your life if you will come to Him today.

Facing Yourself

Luke 15:11-32

Introduction

    A. Honestly facing ourselves is one of the hardest steps we can ever take. Admitting that I need help, something is wrong in my life is very difficult. We are trained for self-protection and preservation—not self-evaluation.

    B. A very familiar story illustrates what happens when we face ourselves honestly. Read Luke 15:11-32.

        1. Normally, we use this passage to inform the unsaved of God's love regardless of how deeply they have sunken into sin. That truth is found here, and it is beautiful. There is another truth that we will add to the first truth.

        2. While one brother came to himself and made improvements, the other brother maintained his righteous pride and lived on in misery. The truth is simple. Making the most of our lives comes from an honest appraisal of our true condition.

I. The Faulty Appraisal of the Younger Brother

    A. He thought that the problem was with his home and parents. Many assume that the Christian life is too boring. The younger brother had a faulty concept of the true problem.

    B. His look into the distance was faulty. The far country looked great from a distance.

    C. He assumed that the people over there had the answers to life. He soon discovered that was not true. What had looked and sounded so good from a distance became garbage up close. He also learned that those he thought would be good friends were self-absorbed.

II. Correct Decisions by the Younger Brother (v. 17)

    A. He made three decisions:

1. He decided that the pigpen was a terrible way of life. Something had to be better.
2. He took the first step to correct the situation (v. 18).
3. The bad things of a good life are better than the best things of a bad life.

B. After making an honest appraisal he knew that it was time for him to act (v. 20). His father could not come into his environment, but he could leave and go home.

C. The positive results of his decision are obvious (vv. 20-24). He found that the good life comes from personal introspection and change.

III. Faulty Perspective of the Elder Brother

A. He was as miserable in his self-righteousness as his younger brother was in his sinful lifestyle. He could represent a lot of church people. He had a more difficult time facing his needs than his brother did in facing his. He never did anything outrageous—no prostitutes, no pigpen.

B. His problem was two fold. A person cannot love others and still act as he did in verse 28. He had too much self-love (v. 29).

C. He assumed that the father should not love his wayward brother. Genuine love never shoots its wounded.

D. The greatest tragedy of this story is the elder brother's failure to come to himself. He missed the celebration because of his attitude.

Conclusion

A. When we come to ourselves our Heavenly Father celebrates.

B. Jesus was sent by the Father to speak to our hearts today so that we do not need to miss the heavenly celebration.

C. Today, make an honest appraisal of yourself and accept His grace so that you can enjoy the celebration.

He Waits!

Revelation 3:20

Introduction

   A. In the Book of Revelation, John is in exile on the Isle of Patmos.
      1. On Patmos God revealed to John many things that are vital to our eternal destiny. The message includes words to the seven churches along with descriptions of judgment, heaven, and hell.
      2. God did this to make every effort to bring humankind into the Kingdom. In the midst of his message to the church at Laodicea is a statement of promise that is vital to all of us. Read the text: Rev. 3:20.
   B. God wants our attention.
      1. "Here I am" simply states that something important is about to be revealed. Look at some other uses of this same salutation. *a)* To Mary in Luke 1:28; *b)* From John the Baptist to the crowd in John 1:29; *c)* To the believers in 1 John 3:1.
      2. In each case it is the announcement that something vital is being communicated to the listeners. Consider this message.

I. "I Stand at the Door and Knock"

   A. It is God who wants to be admitted into our hearts.
      1. We either accept or reject God—not just a church or a pastor.
      2. God is putting forth a personal effort to be our friend.
   B. God is knocking at the doors of our hearts.
      1. He makes the effort that we should be putting forth. He takes the initiative in seeking us. He is the Good Shepherd searching for the lost sheep.
      2. We should be seeking Him. He is the door to the sheepfold. He is the way to the Father.
      3. Note how careful He is to make sure that the Person

knocking is not a stranger. His sheep respond to His voice (John 10).

II. "If Anyone Hears My Voice and Opens the Door, I Will Come In"
A. He will not open the door.
1. The only latch is on the inside.
2. We must open the door if we want to be His friend.
B. How long will He wait? Who knows? He is patient, but His patience ultimately does come to an end (see Rom. 1).

III. "And Eat with Him and He with Me" (He Wants to Fellowship with Us)
A. He wants to be our friend.
1. Like He was with Adam before he betrayed Him in Gen. 3.
2. Like He was with Enoch in Gen. 5.
3. Like He was with His disciples, especially Peter, James, and John.
B. It is a joy to share meals with friends.
1. When we dine with friends, that indicates we are kindred spirits.
2. Jesus tells us that He wants to fellowship in that way with us.

Conclusion
A. Jesus knocks tenderly at the doors of our hearts, desiring to be our Friend.
B. How long will you make Him wait? Remember, He will not open the door.
C. Keep in mind that He will not stand there forever.
D. Your eternal destiny is in the balance. So, will you open the door of your heart to Him today? He is waiting to come in.

The Rate of Exchange

Matthew 16:26

Introduction

A. The Bible contains many references to the value of the souls of humankind. Read Matt. 16:26. Some other scriptures that speak to this include Matt. 11:29 and 22:37. There are approximately 500 sentences in which "soul" is the subject.

B. What is the soul of humankind? It is the eternal part of each one of us. It is the everlasting breath that is imparted by our Creator God (Gen. 2:7). The soul is the real, eternal part of each one of us that never ceases to exist.

C. Jesus asked a question that everyone needs to consider seriously.
1. What kind of a bargain is it if we get everything we want here but in the process we lose our eternal lives?
2. Jesus is telling us that we need to consider what we are receiving here for what we are giving up for all of eternity.

D. There are two serious thoughts to consider: (1) the soul can be lost; (2) the world cannot be gained.

I. All of Us Exchange Our Souls for Something

A. Look at the story of Esau in Gen. 25.
1. Esau thought he would die without eating immediately. He would not have died.
2. He thought that the food would satisfy him. It did not. It just touched his hunger.
3. He probably believed that he could reverse the exchange later. He could not.

B. Today, many people are following Esau's example. They are driven by a desire that cannot be permanently satisfied. They are deserted by satisfactions that are only temporary.

C. Many young people have chosen to follow the cycle of destruction. They are trying alcohol, dope, sex—anything to satisfy their physical drives. When they are deserted by their physical drives, they feel hopeless and defeated.

D. The adult world is no better than the young people of today's world. Many seek fulfillment in material possessions, alcohol, and social standing, but these things do not solve the deep needs and hungers within them. A poor bargain is a bad bargain whether it is made by young people or adults.

II. There Is Something Worthy of Our Very Best

A. To young people, Jesus offers a reason to live.

1. He was a revolutionary in the world of His day. He tore down the hypocrisy and deceit of the establishment at that time. He offered a replacement of purity, sincerity, honesty, and genuine love.

2. Young people who want a better world in which to live must come to Jesus. He provided for a better world through His death on the Cross. Jesus is the Prince of Peace and the Supreme Example of love.

B. To adults, Jesus offers help to make their remaining lives meaningful.

1. Many adults complain about the evil conditions that exist in our world.

2. While they complain about what others do, they sell their own souls for the "pottage" of the physical world.

3. We have no right to complain about anything if we sell our soul to this world.

Conclusion

The eternal question that Jesus asked in our text is critical to us today. Esau learned a hard lesson in Gen. 27:38. What kind of exchange will you make?

Paradise Lost—Paradise Regained

Luke 2:41-52

Introduction

    A. John Milton, one of the famous English poets of the 17th century, wrote many poems. But the greatest of all were two he wrote near the end of his life, *Paradise Lost* and *Paradise Regained.* In *Paradise Lost* he wrote about the fall of humankind from fellowship with God. Losing that fellowship means that paradise is lost. In *Paradise Regained* he pointed to the plan of salvation that restores us to fellowship with God. Therefore, paradise is regained. In both poems paradise is shown to be fellowship with God.

    B. In our scripture for today two of God's good people lost paradise and regained it. Read Luke 2:41-52. In Mary and Joseph's situation as well as in our lives, the presence of Jesus is the key to paradise.

I. Paradise Is the Presence of Jesus

    A. Paradise represents a well-lived life.

        1. There is a state of peace, contentment, security, happiness, and joy. All of these are found in the presence of Jesus Christ.

        2. Jesus: *a)* is the Prince of Peace; *b)* meets every need of our lives, and that gives us security; *c)* wipes away our tears of sorrow, *d)* wants people to be happy (look at His first miracle in John 2.

        3. Paradise is being where Jesus is. Just ask anyone who has spent time with Him.

    B. I love to be in His presence. There is not a problem in my life for which He does not have an answer. There are no needs that He cannot supply. When my heart is heavy He brings healing. When I am with Him, all is well.

II. Paradise Can Be Lost

    A. Mary and Joseph lost Jesus in the midst of legitimate activity—worship.

1. It was the Passover Feast, the highest of Jewish holy days.
2. They lost Jesus while involved in religious activities.
3. This suggests to us that we can lose Him even when we are involved in church activities.

B. They lost Jesus by taking Him for granted (v. 44).
   1. The King James Version reads "supposing." The *New Living Translation* reads "they assumed."
   2. Regardless of the translation, the mistake was in taking His presence for granted.
   3. This was not a sinful act. It was a careless one.

C. This story clearly tells us that we can be good people doing good things and still lose the presence of Jesus.

D. Paradise—Jesus' presence—is lost more often by carelessness than any other reason. It is the slow drifting that causes many people spiritual difficulties (Heb. 2:1).

III. Paradise Can Be Regained

A. Step one is admitting our need. He did not leave them. They left Him (v. 44).

B. Step two comes by seeking Him earnestly (v. 45). They were the losers and had to seek Him. So it is with us. To have Him we must want Him.

C. They found Him where they left Him (v. 46).

Conclusion

Paradise can be ours even in this present age. We cannot afford to take His presence for granted. To those who have lost His presence, He is offering to restore paradise.

Do You Want to Get Well?

John 5:1-14

Introduction

    A. In three and a half years of ministry Jesus gave 30 parables and performed 33 miracles. Parables are miracles of wisdom. Miracles are parables of teaching. Read John 5:1-14.

    B. Look at the setting of this miracle. It took place just inside the Sheep Gate at the pool called Bethesda. His attention was drawn to a man who had been in need for 38 years. Jesus' attention was drawn to the man's obvious frustration in not being healed.

    C. Jesus approached the man with compassion. Jesus asked him, "Do you want to get well?" This may sound like a foolish question, but it is essential to determine if the man was committed to getting well. He did not know Jesus. All he knew was that everything else had failed (v. 7). Jesus gave him a simple command in verse 8.

    D. The Pharisees were not happy with what happened (vv. 9-10).

    E. To follow the story, the man went home, put up his bed, and returned to the Temple to worship for the first time in 38 years (v. 14).

    F. Let us examine what the miracle says to us today.

I. The Miracles of Jesus Depend upon Our Response of Faith

    A. Jesus recognized the royalty of the human will.

        1. Note verse 6.

        2. Unless we want to get well, nothing will be done.

        3. If we really want help, nothing can prevent God's power from helping us.

    B. The man recognized his hopelessness. We must acknowledge our hopelessness outside of God's grace.

C. Jesus confronts us today with the same question He asked that man.
   1. He is asking if we want to live whole, complete lives.
   2. In order to do that we must turn to Jesus in absolute faith.
   3. Like that man, you may have tried and failed many times.
   4. If you will listen to Jesus, He can heal you of your most crippling disease—sin.

II. Jesus Tells Us What to Do

A. Jesus did not heal the man on the ground. He was healed as he responded to Jesus' command, "Get up! Pick up your mat and walk" (v. 8).
B. Look at the order of events.
   1. "Get up" was the one thing this man could not do. It seemed to be an impossible and unreasonable command. The miracle of salvation is the performance of the impossible and unreasonable.
   2. "Pick up your mat and walk" were commanding words. Jesus makes no provision for failure. Today, many people make provision for failure.
   3. "Walk" tells us that we cannot expect to be babied, coddled, or pushed in a buggy.

Conclusion

A. Jesus met the man in the Temple. He issued a command and a warning (v. 14). He reminded the man he was well. He had been changed, healed, and delivered. In verse 14 He told him to "stop sinning." To continue in sin would be tragic.
B. Do you want to be delivered from the most serious disease in your life—sin? Let Jesus heal you today by exercising your faith in His Word.

God's Great Gift

John 3:14-18

Introduction

    A. John 3:16 is probably the most familiar verse in the Bible. In order to catch the total depth of this message, we must consider the context of this verse—its beauty and promise. Read John 3:14-18.

    B. This is a message of deliverance that is God's gift to all who will receive it. He offers this gift because of His awesome love for us. Nicodemus, a good religious man, needed more than religion.

I. Look at the Need for Deliverance (v. 14)

    A. Jesus is referring to the story of the children of Israel in Num 21.

        1. They were wandering in the wilderness because they failed to trust God. Aaron and Miriam had died.

        2. The children of Israel had many problems on their journey. They began to complain against God and Moses (Num. 21:4).

        3. God is never vindictive, but He will not tolerate unnecessary complaining and bad attitudes from people for whom He has provided so much. God punished them for their attitudes by sending deadly serpents into their camp. When the people realized their need and asked for forgiveness, God provided help (Num. 21:7-9).

    B. Every person needs help. We become the victims of Satan's enticements as we journey through life. Note these important scriptures: Rom. 3:23; 6:23; 5:8.

    C. Each one of us needs personal deliverance from the serpent's bite.

        1. Sin is absolutely uncontrollable in the lives of humankind.

        2. Illustration: See stories of Samson in Judg. 16 and of King Saul in 1 Sam. 28.

3. In the same way that each person in the Israelite camp had to look in faith in order to be saved, so must we.

II. Look at the Way to Experience Deliverance (vv. 15-16)

A. Those in the wilderness who exercised faith in God's provision lived. Surely there were some that died through unbelief. God's provision seemed too simple for them.

B. They should have learned that what God promises He can do. They crossed the Red Sea because they had faith in God (Exod. 14). They did not trust God and missed the Promised Land (Num. 13:26—14:4).

C. The key to life for you and me today is to truly take Him at His word. It is the same as when a drowning person takes hold of a raft. Whoever "relies" on Him is like an airplane passenger who depends on the pilot. We need to believe God—not just to believe in God.

III. Look at Why He Delivers Us—Love (v. 16)

A. "Why?" is the eternal question. Again *The Amplified Bible* reads, "God so greatly loved and dearly prized the world." We are a valuable possession to God.

B. Love is the strongest motive in the universe. It compels us to do the impossible because it never lets us give up.

C. Love has no price tag. It never asks what the cost will be. Illustration: When our child is sick we never ask the cost to make our child well.

D. God feels that way about you and me.

Conclusion

A. Look at the results of it all. The best of life now and an eternity to be enjoyed with the Father. There will be no condemnation now or ever (v. 18).

B. We will never understand why God loves us like He does. We can only experience this love by receiving God's great gift of Jesus as our personal Savior.

The Eternal Decision

Matthew 27:15-22

Introduction

A. Today's scripture is one of the most serious texts in the Bible. It speaks of the eternal decision that faces each one of us. It is not eternal because I have plenty of time to make it but because it determines my eternal destiny. Like a magnifying glass that can focus sunlight, this text focuses our attention on an inescapable decision. Read Matthew 27:15-22.

B. There is another text mentioned in the context of our scripture text. In verse 17 the crowd was called upon to make that decision. There is much that could be preached at this point about the price our society pays for the decisions we have made to choose something other than Christ.

C. In the final analysis my personal decision is the most important thing. My life may be affected by a public decision, but my eternal destiny is affected by my personal decision. Since this is such a critical area, we look at the greatest decision we ever make.

I. There Are Many Options Available to Us in Life

A. There are decisions on matters of personal relationships. What kind of person am I going to be? My personality can be trained. What will I do with my life? The choice is mine. Who will be my life companion? All of us want happy homes. These and other decisions are important but only affect this life.

B. The decision I make concerning my relationship with Jesus is crucial. It will have a definite effect on everything I do in this life. Of greater importance, it determines my eternal destiny. I can make adjustments for failure in this life. I cannot adjust eternity.

II. This Is a Personal Decision to Be Made

A. Pilate was asking for advice in his personal decision (v. 22). He asked the wrong crowd. He did not need their advice. As a Roman ruler he could do whatever he chose. He was looking for an excuse to make a bad decision.

B. Today, many people try to escape taking personal responsibility for decisions. Some blame their bad decisions on their background. Some blame social circumstances in which they live. Some try to blame their failure on the influence of others.

C. The real issue is, "What will I do with Jesus?"

III. This Is an Inescapable Decision

A. Pilate tried to excuse himself. He attempted to wash away his responsibility (v 24). He tried to prepare an excuse so that he could say, "I tried to prevent it." According to his own statement, he had the ability to release Jesus (John 19;10).

B. This decision for each one of us is inescapable.
   1. Nothing you can do or say can ever change your responsibility for a decision concerning your relationship with Jesus Christ.
   2. Many people try to delay making that decision.
   3. Seriously consider this. If Jesus should come or should you go, your decision for eternity has been made.
   4. Eternity waits for no one. Illustration: The tragic explosion of the space shuttle sent seven people into eternity without any warning.

Conclusion

A. The eternal question is simple, "What shall I do with Jesus?" It is unavoidable, and it can never be changed. Pilate was condemned for his decision.

B. Today this is your decision. What will you do with Jesus?

God Speaks

Hebrews 1:1-3; 2:1-4

Introduction

A. God spoke to the people in the Old Testament in a variety of ways. He spoke audibly to Noah (Gen. 6 and 7). He spoke to Jacob through the vision of a ladder (Gen. 28). He spoke to Moses through a burning bush (Exod. 3). He spoke to Balaam through a donkey (Num. 22:21). He spoke to Samuel in a quiet voice when he was a little boy (1 Sam. 3).

B. When He speaks to us through His Son, Jesus Christ, it is critical that we listen. Read Heb. 1:1-3; 2:1-4). By listening and obeying the voice of God the Old Testament characters were blessed. They knew God's plan for their lives. By listening to Jesus, we know God's plans for our lives.

C. I believe this passage makes this message even more valuable to us. God is saying that He wants to be sure we understand His love for us. He is telling us that He wants us to experience what He had in mind at creation.

D. Through Jesus, God shows us who we really were created to be—His highest order of creation—His image in the flesh.

I. Look at the Problem

A. Adam and Eve sinned. They created a major problem for all of us. Sin deprives us of fellowship with the Father.

B. God created us for a warm, loving relationship with Him.
   1. By their actions Adam and Eve said, "Nothing doing!"
   2. God did not give up. He started a plan to restore His highest creation to fellowship.

C. God would not abandon the children into which He had put so much of himself.
   1. Illustration: As parents, we love our children even when they are rebellious.

23

2. It is the same way with God. He reaches out, calls and cares because he loves us.

II. The Bible is Not About Sin; It Is About Restoration

A. The primary message is that God loves us and has plans for us. He tells us if we will listen to His Son, He will show us how to enjoy life now and paradise for eternity.
B. The author of Hebrews wrote this book to lift up Jesus.
1. Jesus was a better deliverer than Moses (Heb. 3). Moses led them out of Egypt. Jesus leads us from a harder taskmaster—sin. Jesus is a better high priest (Heb. 7).
2. Old Testament priests went into the holy of holies seeking forgiveness. Jesus sits at the Father's right hand interceding for us (Heb. 8). Jesus offered a better sacrifice (Heb. 9).
3. Old Testament priests offered the blood of bulls and goats that provided temporary relief from the guilt of sin. Jesus offered His own blood for us to provide permanent relief from sin. Jesus offers a better freedom (Heb. 10).
4. People who listen to Him are set free to become what God had in mind in the beginning. God's light shines through the darkness of a sinful world to lift us into His glorious presence.
C. God's fingerprints are all over us. Through Jesus, He is trying to lift us into a special experience (chap. 4).

Conclusion

A. God speaks to us through His Son, Jesus. What will your answer be?
B. Because He listened, Noah floated on the top of disaster, Moses led his people out of slavery, and Gideon won an incredible victory.
C. God is still speaking today. The question is, "Are you listening?"
D. Do not forget the warning of 2:1-4.

The Great Folly

Luke 12:13-21

Introduction

A. Somewhere, sometime, all of us decide what is most important in our lives. It is critical that we choose something that will not fail us.

B. Unfortunately, we live in a make-believe world. We are exposed to a lot of fantasy and make-believe, where everything somehow works. Many people adopt this approach for their lives. In reality, everything does not work out pleasantly and successfully. There are some things in life that are beyond our control. Because of that, no one can live independent of everything and everyone else.

C. Jesus underscores this truth with the parable of the rich fool. Read Luke 12:13-21. This man was apparently successful. Yet Jesus called him a fool. While no bad habits or serious sins were evident, Jesus said he was foolish. He played the part of a fool by the things he forgot. This cost him his eternal life. The man in our scripture did the reverse.

I. He Forgot Other People

A. This man thought of no one but himself. Notice that he said "I" six times and "my" five times. It is obvious that this man's life was centered entirely around himself.

B. Through the ages, philosophers have emphasized that no person is an island. Anyone who permits personal interests to dominate his or her life is like this man.

II. He Forgot That a Man Is More than What He Owns

A. The man in the parable saw life only in terms of material possessions. He failed to distinguish between what a person has and what a person is.

B. People who have all that life can offer but no inner joy are prime targets for misery.

III. He Forgot Who Is the True Source of Happiness

A. He had a false concept of life and did not know what it takes to make us happy. He was like the man in Eccles. 2:1-11. Note verses 10 and 11.

B. While money can buy a lot of things, it cannot buy a sense of usefulness, a clear conscience, and a contented mind. Happiness is the result of everything on the inside being on the Lord's side.

IV. He Forgot God

A. His greatest blunder was in failing to put God first. There was nothing wrong with greater barns and enjoying life. The mistake that he made was in leaving God out of his plans.

B. Today, many people are still leaving God out of their plans. We must remember that we have an appointment with God (James 4:13-15).

C. He made his plans to live many years. He should have taken another step and made plans to die. At the height of his earthly success he had no choice—he left it all.

D. We deceive ourselves when we assume we have plenty of time.

   1. The devil does not say, "You will not die." He tells us that we will not die soon.

   2. While we do not need to live under the cloud of death we do need to recognize the reality of death. The persons who prepare for it are wise.

   3. Illustration: World Trade Center tragedy where many unsuspecting people died.

Conclusion

The greatest folly of our day is that many people live like this fool giving no thought to God and the fact that they will someday cross the line of worlds. Remember Him. Make plans for a great life, but be sure to remember God.

THE PRECIOUS PROMISE RECEIVED

2 Corinthians 6:14—7:1

Introduction

  A. God has given many wonderful promises to humankind. Some promises were received with joy, such as the deliverance from Egypt. Some were missed with sorrow, such as the Israelites' failure to enter Canaan. The scripture for today offers one of the greatest promises of all. Read 2 Cor. 6:14—7:1.

  B. A promise must be received before its value can be realized. Illustration: A promise is like a check. It is not good until it is endorsed. All promises have some provisions that bring them to fulfillment. This text points out some of the provisions for the wonderful promise of verse 18.

I. Notice the Requirement for Separation in This Passage (vv. 14-16a)

  A. The call for division begins in these verses. A person cannot live on both sides of the issue.

    1. J. B. Phillips translated this: "Don't link up with unbelievers and try to work with them." There is no common bond between good and evil.

    2. Many Christians try to live on both sides. This cannot be done. Jesus speaks strongly to this issue in Matt. 6:24.

    3. The Hebrews were forbidden to unite materials or animals of different kinds. In the same way the nature of a believer is different from that of a nonbeliever.

  B. After telling them that they could not be on both sides, God invites us to come to Him (vv. 16-18). These promises are made for those who are separated to God.

  C. In 7:1 Paul writes that these promises are for us as well.

II. Take a Closer Look at the Promises Given (v. 16b)

  A. Look at the significance of this promise.

1. As long as God is with us, we will have no fear.
2. He will provide for us in the same way that He provided for the Israelites.
B. "I will receive you kindly and treat you with favor" (v. 17*b*, AMP.). God makes an incredible difference in the lives of those He favors. We pray and ask God to bless. Here He promises those things to those who are separated to Him.
C. "You will be my sons and daughters" (v. 18). It is natural for parents to want the very best for their children. God is able and will provide the very best for His children.

III. Look at the Means to Activate the Promises (7:1)
A. The first step is to purify ourselves. This means getting rid of everything that contaminates and defiles. Separation from all sinful activities is vital to enjoying God's best.
B. The second step is to cultivate holiness.
1. We are not to just put off sin. We are to pursue holiness out of reverence for God.
2. Follow Christ's example as stated by Paul in Phil. 2:5-8.
3. Jesus modeled this in the Garden through His total submission to the Father (Matt. 26:39).
C. The "perfection of holiness" will set us apart for sacred use by God. We become like the vessels of the Temple—fit to be used for His glory. We become like the disciples—vessels for His message to change our world.

Conclusion
Paul challenges us to be what Jesus died for us to be—Children of God. Will you accept the provisions that Jesus made when he died? (Heb. 13:12). Don't miss out on this precious promise. Receive it today.

God's Grace

Titus 2:11-14

Introduction
A. Grace is the foundation of our faith. We talk, teach, and sing about the unmerited, undeserved, favorable treatment that God provides for us through Jesus. We love to sing great songs about grace ("Amazing Grace," "Wonderful Grace of Jesus," "He Giveth More Grace").

B. Such great songs communicate something special to the world. It is not what we are that causes God to love us and treat us with such favor. It is His favor, love, and grace that makes us what we are. The grace of God brings joy, purpose, and peace to our lives today.

C. There are two aspects of grace that we want to look at from today's passage. (1) The grace of God brings salvation to all humankind. (2) The grace of God enables us to live our lives prepared for His coming. Read Titus 2:11-14.

I. Notice God's Initiative in Reaching Out to Humankind
A. God's grace is more clearly demonstrated through Jesus' death on the Cross than anywhere else. No one ever deserved a death of that nature.

B. Look at the physical suffering He endured while hanging on the Cross.
1. His feet that had carried Him on missions of mercy around the world were bound to the Cross by nails.
2. His hands that had wiped away the tears of many, opened their eyes, and lifted awesome burdens were nailed to the Cross. His hands were nailed open as if to signify that He is reaching for you and me.
3. His side was pierced and enough blood flowed to wash away the sins of the entire world.

C. The crowd at the foot of the Cross that day insulted Him (Matt. 27:39-44). The load was heavy enough without

29

verbal abuse, but He endured it. He could have called for help but chose not to do so.

D. Why would God permit, even encourage His Son, to be subjected to this? God had stated, "This is my Son" in Matt. 3:17. How could the Father subject His Son to such cruel treatment? There was no other way to solve the deepest problems of humankind. Paul speaks to God's solution in Ephesians 2:4-10.

II. We Have an Initiative to Respond to God's Grace

A. There are some things from which we withdraw because they are incompatible with the new nature that God gives to us.
   1. We are to deny ungodliness (v. 12). These things that are incompatible with God's holy nature. These things that are forbidden by the Ten Commandments. These things that make us uncomfortable in God's presence.
   2. We are to deny worldly passions.
B. Look at the positive side. Note verses 12-13. They tell us how to live.
   1. We are to live in such a way that is healthy for ourselves and attractive to others. We are to live upright, godly lives in this present world.
   2. Some people do not understand that we can have the ability to live like this. Illustration: Fish caught in water too salty to drink are protected from absorbing the salt. In the same way, God can protect us from our environment if we let Him.
   3. We are to live "godly lives in this present age," which can only be done when the grace of God is present in our lives.

Conclusion

Jesus did His part in providing grace by His suffering and death on the Cross. Will you do your part by receiving Him as your Savior so that the grace of God can bring forgiveness, peace, and joy to your life?

Basics of Being a Christian

John 3:1-17

Introduction
- A. We are looking at one of the most familiar passages in the New Testament. Normally we break this passage into two separate pictures. Verses 1-10—we must be born again, and verses 14-17—God's love for the world.
- B. Today, we want to keep everything in the scriptural picture we are examining. There are three basic truths we must understand if we are to become what God wants us to be. Read John 3:1-17.

I. Basic Truth No. 1: Being Religious Is Not Enough to Get a Person to Heaven

- A. Look at the story of Nicodemus.
  1. He was a Pharisee, the supreme religious order of the day. To be a Pharisee one had to be trained in the Old Testament and committed to its keeping.
  2. The word *Pharisee* literally means separated. They were separated to maintain observance of the Law. They knew the Law and emphasized its keeping almost to a fault. It is recorded that on at least one occasion the Pharisees chose to die rather than to fight on the Sabbath Day.
  3. Nicodemus was a member of the Sanhedrin. There were 70 men of the various religious orders that composed the Supreme Court of the Jews. This good, educated religious man needed something else. Note verses 2-3.
- B. What does it mean to be born again? To be born again is a miraculous experience. Our old, sinful, unsatisfied self is changed. (See Paul's statement in 2 Cor. 5:17.) Being religious can be a tragedy. The only way to heaven is by being born again.

II. Basic Truth No. 2: Becoming a Christian Is Simple

A. We have an aversion to simple things. Sometimes the church contributes to the problem of religious complexity. The tendency is to equate being religious with keeping the Law and rituals. Nicodemus did all of these things. Yet, Jesus said he needed something else.

B. Jesus equates the simplicity of being born again with a story from Num. 21. Deliverance was provided for all who had the faith to accept it. Those who looked in faith lived. Those who did not died. Jesus told a seeking Nicodemus that deliverance was provided for him.

C. Eternal life is irrefutably tied to our dependency upon Jesus.

III. Basic Truth No. 3: God Paid a High Price So We Can Be Saved

A. He sent Jesus to die for the forgiveness from our sins (John 3:16).
   1. He came to pay the price for our sins.
   2. The sacrifice for sins had been made when the high priest went into the holy of holies with a perfect lamb.
   3. The perfect Lamb for our forgiveness is the only begotten Son of God.
   4. Jesus is our High Priest. (See Heb. 9:11-14 and 10:16-22.)

B. Do not stop at verse 16. It is important to include verse 17. Many people misunderstand Christianity. They think it takes the joy out of life. Jesus did not come to take joy from life but to give us a reason to enjoy living. (See John 10:10.)

Conclusion

Nicodemus was a good man, but there was an emptiness in his life. Jesus told him how that void in his life could be filled. There are people listening today who are good people but need to be born again. Will you receive what Jesus wants to give to you today?

An Adequate Foundation

Matthew 7:24-27; Psalm 51:7-12

Introduction

    A. No building is more secure than the foundation upon which it is built. In this same way, no life is more secure than its foundation.

    B. In today's scripture Jesus gives us the need for a foundation and David gives us the formula for that. Read the scripture (Matt. 7:24-27; Ps. 51:7-12). David is the architect of an adequate foundation that produces a life of happiness.

I. The First Step in Establishing an Adequate Foundation Is Deliverance from Sin (Ps. 51:1-4)

    A. Sin is the most damaging force in the world. It was sin that destroyed King Saul, the first king of Israel (1 Sam. 15 and 31). Sin nearly destroyed David (2 Sam. 11 and 12). In Ps. 51:2 David asked God to cleanse him from the destruction of sin. In Ps. 103:12 he testified that God answered his prayer.

    B. Sin is still destructive in our world today. Anyone who plays with sin will discover its deceptiveness and destructiveness. Illustration: Sin is to the spiritual being what cancer is to the physical being. It must be dealt with decisively or disaster will follow.

II. The Second Step for Deliverance from Sin Is to Have a Pure Heart (Ps. 51:10)

    A. David had wanted no part of sin. He asked God to purify his inner nature—the source of his life.

    B. We understand that nothing can be clean and dirty at the same time. Impurities in anything always cause trouble.

    C. A right spirit is necessary in order to have an adequate foundation for life.

1. We need a right spirit toward God. He is our Father—not a policeman.
2. We need a right spirit toward the church. It is a privilege to be part of one.
3. We need a right spirit toward others. A healthy respect for others is necessary.
4. We must have a proper awareness of ourselves.
5. If the foundation of our lives is going to be a good one, we must follow David's expressed desire for a clean heart and a right spirit.

III. The Third Step for Deliverance from Our Sins Is to Maintain the Presence of God (Ps. 51:11)

A. The greatest source of strength we can have is the presence of God in our lives. Nothing has ever overcome Him. Illustrations of God's power are many: the Red Sea, the walls of Jericho, and so forth.

B. His presence is our source of assurance. Like the three Hebrew children in Dan. 3, we will also have some fiery furnace experiences. But with Him we, too, can prevail. In John 14:16-17 Jesus promised that He would not only be with us but would be in us as well. This promise means that wherever we are, God is. Wherever God is, there is victory for the believer. With Him, we have a firm foundation under our lives.

Conclusion

A. A person can build a house without putting in a good foundation and save money on the initial cost. But all is lost when the storms come.

B. It is the same way in life. We can build our lives on cheap foundations and pay a terrible price later.

C. Jesus gives us the formula for building our lives on something that will last (Matt. 7:24).

D. What kind of foundation are you putting under your life?

The Three Groups

Matthew 26:36-46

Introduction

  A. On two occasions a garden became a battleground for the souls of humankind. The first time was in the Garden of Eden. There Adam and Eve yielded to sin, and all of the misery, disease, and heartache of the world began. Even in the face of sin and rebellion, God gave a promise (Gen. 3:15). The second time is found in today's scripture passage. Read Matthew 26:36-46.

  B. The question that all of us must answer is, "Where would I be located in the Garden of Gethsemane?" We are going to take a look at the groups and determine the one to which we want to be related.

I. Look at the Difference in Their Positions

  A. All of us classify ourselves.

    1. We are not classified according to degree of education or financial ability.

    2. We are simply classified according to our relationship with Jesus Christ.

    3. Please note that Judas classified himself with Jesus' enemies.

  B. The first group was located near the edge of the garden.

    1. This group represents a large percentage of today's average church members. it has been said that at least 25 percent of members could disappear, and the church would not realize they had left. This group is a picture of the people who want to be in the church but related to the world at the same time.

    2. It is time for the church to clearly declare itself in its relationship with God. Illustration: During the 37-year war between Spain and the Netherlands Prince William of Orange was tempted to betray. He said, "Not for life, nor wife, nor children, nor lands would I mix one drop of the poison of treason in my cup."

When he died, children stopped playing and cried. God help us to be so committed to Christ.

II. Look at the Difference in Size
A. The majority of the crowd is farther away from Jesus and closer to the world.
B. If we could talk to the eight, their response could be interesting. They could not tell us how to find Jesus.
   1. These are some of the same individuals left behind at the foot of the Mount of Transfiguration who caused a father to doubt (Matt. 17:14-16).
   2. Two questions face each of us: Can we tell people how to find Jesus? Do we encourage or discourage their faith?

III. Look at the Difference in Revelation
A. The deepest things of God are reserved for those who are nearest to His heart. Compare verses 6, 38, and 39.
B. If you want God to reveal the deepest mysteries of himself to you, you will have to move into the heart of the garden.

IV. Look at the Difference in Their Assignment
A. To the first group He simply said, "Sit here" (v. 36). Even Judas passed them by when he came looking for the Master. To the second group He shared His burden (v. 38).
B. To the Father, He surrendered everything (v. 39).

Conclusion
Each of us faces the question about where we are located in relation to Jesus. The world needs to see people who are so clearly identified with Jesus that they can find Him through them. Remember, you locate yourself. Where are you today?

Time to Get Serious

Luke 12:1-9; 13:24-30

Introduction

    A. This is Luke's account of the Sermon on the Mount. While it closely parallels Matthew's account, each has a special emphasis. Matthew's emphasis appears to be simple Christian living. Luke's emphasis is a more serious approach to the reality of God, judgment, and eternity.

    B. The world is full of daydreamers. There are many people who fool themselves by thinking they can ignore God. Because they have managed to escape responsibility in other areas of their lives, they think they can do that with God.

    C. In these passages of scripture Jesus is trying to get His listeners to face reality. As a minister of the gospel, it is my desire to do the same thing today. Hear the warnings of the Master today. (Note: Read scripture with points.)

I. A Time of Revealing Will Come (Luke 12:1-3)

    A. Beware of hypocrisy and deceit.

        1. This is religion without reality and power. It is a form of godliness that denies the power of God (2 Tim. 3:5). It is a silent pollution that works until it overtakes a person's life.

        2. The Pharisees were morally good but spiritually corrupt. Jesus warned them to be on their guard. One day our experience with Jesus will be revealed for what it truly is. (See Eccles. 12:14.)

II. A Time to Fear Will Come (Luke 12:4-5)

    A. We must fear Satan in any form. Illustration: Treat him as you treat a communicable disease. We should be more afraid of Satan than we are of people.

    B. Fear him now while you can still do so. You will never be able to control sin. Run from it!

    C. Flee Satan and repent (Luke 13:1-5).

III. A Time to Watch Is Here (Luke 12:37-40)

A. We do not dare to take Jesus Christ's return carelessly. The Bible emphasizes that He will come again (John 14). Wise people will be prepared for His return.

B. His return will cause a separation (Luke 13:24-27). Nothing will matter at that moment except that we are prepared.

IV. A Time of Reward Will Come (Luke 12:8-9)

A. For those who know Jesus personally there will be a great reward. Illustration: In the same way that a person on trial has a defense attorney, Jesus will be our defense before the Judge of the universe.

B. For those who do not know Jesus, it will be a time of reckoning.

1. Those who disown Him here will stand alone in God's judgment hall.

2. Suddenly, they will realize the truth of the Word, but it will be too late to change the outcome.

3. Many may be like the young man Jesus told about in Luke 12:16-21.

Conclusion

A. Please consider the deadly consequences of daydreaming about your experience with God. There is nothing wrong with daydreaming about some things. But not here. Some people think that they can make a change at the last moment. But remember Luke 13:25. This is the same message that we receive from the parable of the ten virgins (Matt. 25:1-13).

B. It is time to wake up, get serious, and face the reality of your true relationship with Jesus Christ. You may face Him sooner than you think. Are you prepared?

A Miracle of Human Transformation

Mark 5:1-20

Introduction
  A. Those who listen and obey God's voice experience a major change in their lives. Each one of us needs a miraculous change that can only come from Jesus. Today's scripture records a miracle that illustrates the change He wants to bring. Read the scripture (Mark 5:1-20).
  B. This passage is very appropriate for the day in which we live. We have tried to clean up sin by changing the languages and making excuses. There is a cycle of sin being perpetuated within our society. Today's miracle shows that God can break that cycle. It teaches us three very important lessons.

I. Lesson One: Sin Is Uncontrollable (vv. 2-4)
  A. The people in this man's society had tried to control the evil in him. He not only harmed other people but also harmed himself. Sin is destructive and becomes more so the longer it is allowed to go on.
  B. Our society is trying to control the evil it has generated.
    1. We have tried many programs, but they soon get old and wear out.
    2. The assumption that money can buy satisfaction and peace is a lie.
    3. We hear about "safe sex," but the truth is only God's plan for sexual abstinence outside of marriage is the only safe sex.
  C. We need a cure for evil not simply something to try to control it. The assumption is that there is no cure. There is a cure through Jesus Christ.
  D. Sin becomes more destructive the longer it is permitted to continue. It is like a cancer that goes untreated—it spreads through the entire being. It is a mistake to assume that sin can be kept "nice." Look at the purpose of sin—to separate us from God. We are living in Rom. 1.

E. We have chaos in our streets and homes because of our attitude toward sin. Sin is uncontrollable by human efforts to manage it.

II. Lesson Two: Jesus Can Cure the Problem (vv. 13-15)

A. Jesus does not give evil one inch of tolerance. He came to defeat sin and He did. No one was beyond His grace. Illustration: Share the story of the woman at the well in John 4.

B. That was then. How about now? No one is beyond the saving grace of our Lord Jesus Christ. Illustration: Tell the story of someone he delivered (Chuck Colson, etc.). The scars of our sins remain. The longer people live in sin, the more scarred their lives will become.

III. Lesson Three: Society Has a Poor Sense of Values (vv. 16-17)

A. Why were the people unhappy when a human being had been salvaged?
   1. Money was more important to them than a person.
   2. Illustration: Paul ran into the same problem in Philippi (Acts 16).

B. Today's society reacts in much the same way.
   1. Pornography thrives on legal maneuvering.
   2. Sex on TV and in the movies is accepted.
   3. There are many areas where the products of sin are of greater value than humans.

Conclusion

A. These truths are very critical to the day in which we live and our personal lives. Sin is uncontrollable, but it is curable through Jesus Christ.

B. Jesus wants to perform a miracle of transformation in your life and our society.

C. Will you let Him perform His miracle in your life today?

The High Cost of Sin

Romans 1:18-32

Introduction

A. The Bible is filled with illustrations of people who learned the hard way that sin carries a high price tag. Illustrations: King Saul, Samson, David, and Judas. Our society has worked hard at bringing the biblical condemnation of sin to an acceptable level. We have attempted to relieve the personal guilt that sin brings.

B. The Bible is the standard of responsibility against which we will be measured. It is the biblical standard (not the social one) that determines our eternal destiny. Every person is a moral creature that will either enjoy the pleasures of heaven or the punishments of hell. There are only two options—God's way or sin's way.

C. 2 Cor. 5:19 reads: "God was reconciling the world to himself in Christ." God enables all who accept Jesus to live in a way that pleases Him. Sin is expensive. Those who fail to come to the Cross and follow Jesus are left to their own devices, and the consequences of a sinful life. In today's scripture Paul describes the cost of the sinful life. Read Rom. 1:18-32.

I. The Bible Clearly Demonstrates the Seriousness of Sin

A. Look at verse 18. God has no patience with sin. While God is love, He is not just love. He offers love to the repentant or justice to the rebellious.

B. Verses 24-29 hold frightening possibilities.
1. Beginning at verse 24, Paul speaks to all kinds of immorality.
2. In verse 29, Paul goes beyond immorality to a frightening picture.
3. This is a serious picture of the outcome of sin.
4. Not one of us wants to be a part of a society like that described in verse 29.

C. The Bible gives many illustrations of God's attitude toward sin.
   1. While almost everyone in Sodom and Gomorrah were guilty of the same lifestyle, God did not change His attitude (Gen. 19). Look at the severity of His attitude toward sin as described in Num. 15.
   2. Look at the response to Achan's sin in Josh. 7. It is important to note that in each instance the entire family and community of the sinner suffered.
D. According to His Word, sin was a very serious matter with God.

II. What Has Changed?
A. God's Word has not changed.
   1. It is still the standard against which we will be measured.
   2. Multiplications of violations of God's law will not change the outcome.
B. The processes of sin have not changed.
   1. Sin may seem to begin innocently but constantly craves more satisfaction.
   2. Paul tells us the payoff for sin in Rom. 6:23.

III. Is There a Solution?
A. Yes—the forgiveness of Jesus and living the Christian lifestyle. Christians keep the commandments. Living this way solves the ugliness as described in verses 29-31.
B. This may seem to be an oversimplification, but it is true. Accepting Jesus is the alternative to paying the high price of sinful living.

Conclusion
None of us wants to pay the high cost of sin as described in this scripture. Sin as a lifestyle is a slippery slope that carries a high price tag. The only alternative is to give our hearts to Jesus Christ and live His way.

The Truth About Sin

Isaiah 53

Introduction

A. Society is beginning to show signs of honesty in dealing with a major problem. Thousands of lives have been destroyed by a disease that was unknown several years ago—AIDS. We have sought and found help in dealing with other crippling diseases. The difference with AIDS is that it originated with a sinful lifestyle but now impacts the lives of many innocent people. This disease is so destructive that it deserves intense research for a solution.

B. There is another disease that is very much like AIDS in character and danger. That disease is sin—the source of all the heartaches and problems of humankind. Sin is not an innocent illness that merely makes us uncomfortable anymore than AIDS is like a common cold. The nature of sin is totally destructive to the best there is in each of us.

C. No one who understands the facts about AIDS deliberately chooses it. This should be our attitude toward sin. We are going to look at three important facts about sin. Today's scripture serves as the foundation of our study. Read Isaiah 53.

I. Fact No. 1: Sin Is Extremely Deceitful

A. It was deceit that sowed the seeds of sin in the beginning. Look at the story of Adam and Eve in Gen. 3. Eve did not know where Satan was leading her. She did know that it was contrary to God's plan.

B. Sin usually starts in a very subtle way.
   1. No one ever starts out to become an alcoholic or a murderer.
   2. An erosion of principles and standards leads to a plunge into depravity. Illustration: See Paul's description in Rom. 1.

C. The temptation of Jesus illustrates the deceitfulness of sin. See. Matt. 4. This illustrates that sin cannot produce what it seems to promise.

II. Fact No. 2: Sin Is Totally Destructive

A. The Bible gives extensive coverage to this truth.
   1. Look at the cost of sin upon Noah's world (Gen. 6—7).
   2. Look at the high price Paul described in Rom. 1:20-29.
   3. The history of our inhumanity to each other testifies to the destructiveness of sin.
B. Sin is still totally destructive. We wrestly constantly with the problems that sin costs in our society. Illustrate with current news stories of drugs, murder, rape, and so forth.
C. The problem our society faces is that we want to make sin sophisticated and nice.
   1. There is no honest way to clean up sin and eliminate its consequences.
   2. Sin is totally destructive. That is its nature. Only God can change that.

III. Fact No. 3: There Is a Cure for Sin

A. The picture would be bleak except for this truth. Isaiah points out that this is why Jesus would come into the world. Jesus came to deliver us from sin. Look at the price He would pay (vv. 5-7).
B. Look at the cure He would provide (v. 12).
C. The New Testament emphasizes this truth. See Paul's statement in Eph. 2:1-6. See Paul's testimony in Gal. 2:20.

Conclusion

If someone could provide a proven cure for cancer, heart disease, or some other serious illness, everyone would want to take advantage of it. A cure for the most serious problem for humankind has been provided. Will you accept Jesus and let Him cure the sin problem in your life?

THE VOICE OF GOD

Hebrews 3:7-19

Introduction

A. This is one of the great passages that should be read frequently by everyone who wants to go to heaven. At some point in every person's life, God speaks. Those who listen and respond to Him are blessed. Those who do not pay a high price for their failure to give heed to His voice.

B. There are many people throughout the Bible who were blessed by God and used for His honor because they listened to His voice. We read about Noah in Gen. 6—8; Moses in Exod. 3; Samuel in 1 Sam. 3; Paul in Acts 9. This list could go on and on.

C. The voice of God is His guidance to lead us to the center of His will for our lives. Without God's voice we are like an airplane without instruments. We are not clearly led through life's journey.

D. All of us need to listen to the voice of God. Read Heb. 3:7-19.

I. Look at the Possibility of Hearing (v. 7)

A. The emphasis is very clear that God is speaking in our world. Illustration: There are many radio stations on the air but only those who are listening hear what they are broadcasting. God is speaking because He has special plans for each one of us.

B. The emphasis of this verse places the responsibility on the listener.

1. According to Heb. 1, God still speaks to those who are listening.

2. Wise persons set their minds and hearts to receive God's voice and guidance. There are many voices clamoring for our attention. God's voice is the one that really matters.

II. Look at the Wisdom of Listening to His Voice (v. 15)

A. Two times in this scripture the urgency of paying attention to God is emphasized.

   1. Verses 12 and 13 issue strong admonitions to the urgency of listening now.

   2. Illustration: The voice of God is analogous to the channel markers that guide great ships in and out of safe harbor. This is a clear message of God's desire to lead us to the safety of His will.

B. Today is the day of salvation. There will never be a tomorrow. It is always today. Those who wait for tomorrow will miss out on the plans that God has for them.

III. Look at the Responsibility We Have to Respond Positively (vv. 16-19)

A. The scripture is very clear about where the responsibility lies for enjoying God's blessings.

   1. The Israelites were unable to enter the Promised Land because they failed to take the responsibility to obey God's guidance (Exod. 13—14).

   2. God had better plans for the Israelites than they had for themselves. They failed to remember the verification of His promises through the early years of the Exodus (vv. 7-11). Note the account God gives in Deut. 29:1-15.

B. The scripture indicates that we may or may not respond to God. God will not force himself upon anyone. The option of listening to God and obeying His voice is an individual choice.

Conclusion

When we hear the voice of God it is very critical that we obey Him. Those who do not heed His voice are like those described in verses 16-19. Are you listening to the voice of Jesus as He calls you to the great life the Father had in mind when He created you?

Cleaning Our Nets

Luke 5:1-11

Introduction

A. In this passage of scripture Jesus is gathering His team. These people are the ones in whom He will entrust the gospel for the world. Read Luke 5:1-11. It is much more meaningful to gather that which (people) has eternal value rather than that which (fish) has temporary value. Jesus chose these men because they were simple, hard-working, and took good care of their equipment (v. 2). They responded quickly to their opportunity (v. 11).

B. God wants you and me to be fishers of people. The nets we will use are lives. In order to be effective our nets must be in good condition. Illustration: Many fishermen have lost great fish because they did not take time to check their equipment. Many people may be lost because professing Christians have faulty equipment.

C. To be effective, let us, like the men in our scripture who checked their fishing equipment, check our spiritual equipment.

I. Don't Be Surprised If We Find Some Poor Attitudes and Feelings

A. We may find jealousy and envy.

1. We will not be able to relax in the spirit while mentally wrestling with our attitudes toward someone else. How could we ever be jealous of someone else when God has already been better to us than we ever deserved?

2. Jealousy and envy restrict the flow of love we must have to reach others.

B. Judgment and criticism will surely foul our nets. Look at the words of Jesus in Matt. 7:1-2. It is a fact that where love is thick faults are thin.

C. An attitude of unforgiveness will certainly foul our nets. Jesus taught forgiveness (see Matt. 18:21-22). Follow Jesus' example (see Luke 23:34). Paul taught forgiveness (see Eph. 4:32 and Col. 3:12-13).

D. Poor attitudes and feelings can be destructive to our efforts to reach others.
   1. Healthy Christians like healthy bodies quickly surround and expel infections.
   2. If we intend to be "fishers of men" we must eliminate these things from our nets.

II. Don't Be Surprised If "Closet Sins" Get Caught in Your Net

A. It would be miraculous if there is no one present who has something hidden in their lives. The Bible is clear on this issue (see Eccles. 12;14 and Luke 12:2-3).

B. Secret sins make their victims miserable.
   1. They can be the language we use, gossip, or questionable business practices, and so forth.
   2. Would it surprise some of your acquaintances that you are a Christian?
   3. Does the way you live encourage or discourage those around you to accept Jesus?
   4. What kind of mind games do you play while watching TV or using the Internet?

Conclusion

A. If I have made some of you uncomfortable, that was my intention. We need to repair our nets before they become a major problem.

B. Jesus is passing by today to invite all of us to be fishers of people. What is the condition of your net? Are there poor attitudes that need to be addressed? What about sin? Jesus is gathering people today to follow Him to spread the Good News to our world. We have an opportunity. Join me in checking our nets in preparation to be obedient to the opportunity that Jesus is giving to us.

Joy for the Journey

John 15:9-17

Introduction

    A. On the last night of His life, Jesus prepared His disciples to carry on His work. He gave an example of the way they were to live—to serve others (chap. 13). He gave them hope (chap. 14). He gave them their assignment—to bear fruit (chap. 15). He gave them the promise of the Holy Spirit (chap. 16). He prayed for them (chap. 17).

    B. Right in the midst of these chapters, Jesus spoke of one of the greatest needs of those who follow Him—that they would have joy. Read John 15:9-17. Note verse 11. Genuine joy is one of the most attractive traits of Christianity. It is genuine joy that shines like headlights in a dark, dangerous world. Jesus wants believers to experience the joy that He knew.

I. Take a Look at the Joy of Jesus

    A. He came into the world to carry out His Father's will, and He did that.

        1. The Jews had looked at God with fear (Deut. 6:1; 31:12).

        2. Jesus looked at the Father with favor. Note Jesus' response to the disciples in John 4:31-34.

    B. Jesus built a bridge between God and humans so we may enjoy the Father's presence. The Cross is our bridge to fellowship with our Heavenly Father. It is our bridge to life now and for eternity.

    C. Look at Jesus' journey. Jesus enjoyed being with people (Matt. 9:11).

        1. Children were attracted to Him (Mark 10:13-16).

        2. He was "a man of sorrows, and familiar with suffering" (Isa. 53:3). But He did not gather a following by being morose.

    D. People are attracted to a joyful experience. Illustration: No one is ever attracted to a funeral procession, but many people will crash parties because of the fun that is happening.

II. How Do We find Joy?
A. By having absolute faith in God.
 1. The level of our pleasure in life will be in direct proportion to our faith in His Word.
 2. We can trust Him with the stuff that others struggle with (see Prov. 3:5-6).
B. By making a total commitment to His will. Note God's plans in Isa. 1:19; Hab. 1:5; Jer. 29:11.
 1. In the garden Jesus prayed, "not my will, but yours be done" (Luke 22:42). The Father's will caused Him to be crucified, but it also resurrected Him.
 2. We may have some tough experiences, but He will ultimately give us joy. Illustration: Once you have survived a fiery furnace or lion's den, you lose your fear of them.

III. God Intended for Life to Be a Joyful Journey
A. Remember your traveling Companion. Your Companion is the same One who created the world. He is the same One who has never lost a battle. He is the One who has unlimited resources. He is the One who loved you enough to die for you.
B. Joy for the journey will not come from just being religious. Illustration: The rich young man in Matt. 19:16-22.
C. God wants each one of us to enjoy life's journey. By pursuing the Father's will, Jesus experienced joy. Likewise, by pursuing the Father's will, we can experience joy as well.

Conclusion
Jesus invites each one of us to join Him in the journey of life so that we can experience the joy that He provided through His death on the Cross. Will you follow Jesus' example and experience the joyful life God wants to provide for you?

Lessons from a Rich Young Man

Mark 10:17-22

Introduction

    A. A study of the nameless persons in the New Testament is interesting. In John 6, we read about the boy who gave his lunch to Jesus and 5,000 people were fed. This encourages us to know that anyone can be used by Jesus. In Luke 7, we read about the widow of Nain who was comforted by Jesus. This demonstrates that all of us are candidates to benefit from His presence. In John 5, we read about the healing of the man by the pool. This demonstrates to us that no condition is beyond Jesus' control.

    B. These nameless people along with many others could represent many in this congregation.

    C. Unfortunately, there is another unknown person with whom many identify. Read Mark 10:17-22. This young man teaches us some vital lessons.

I. Lesson One: Being Religious Does Not Qualify Us for Heaven

    A. This young man was very religious. His question shows that he had a religious heart (v. 17). It was a noble question revealing his hunger for a deep, lasting relationship.

    B. He recognized something special in Jesus. Notice his approach in verse 17. He was beyond the level of unbelievers but peace eluded him.

    C. There are a multitude of good people who do not know the peace that Jesus offers.

       1. Jesus spoke to many of them in Matt. 7:21.

       2. In James 1:22 we are admonished to get beyond just being religious.

       3. The Bible does not call us to "goodness." We are called to godliness.

4. This young man represents a host of religious people who do not have peace.

II. Lesson Two: Material Possessions Do Not Produce Peace

A. Note the description of this young man in verse 22. We read in Mark 10:22 that he had great wealth. In Luke 18:22 we read that he was a ruler. This young man represents those people who are well supplied with what the world considers to be necessary for happiness.

B. Material possessions do not produce peaceful lives today. A look at the daily newspaper shows that many wealthy people are miserable. The absence of material possessions does not automatically produce peace. Material things have nothing to do with giving or taking away eternal life.

C. This young man kept the "things" he had at the price of the peace that he sought. Note verse 22. How long did he have his "riches"? Perhaps 50 years? How long did he forfeit peace? Forever.

III. Lesson Three: Jesus Makes No Compromise for Anyone

A. This young man could be a credit to any church. Jesus requires total commitment. Total commitment was the price for the power of Pentecost. There is no room in God's kingdom for half-hearted Christians.

B. Today, it takes total commitment to know spiritual success and peace. There are no boundary lines in the lives of true believers. Jesus will not share our hearts. He will be Lord of all or not Lord at all.

Conclusion

What must we do to have eternal life? We must accept Jesus' terms by giving Him first place in our lives. Those who do what Jesus tells them to do live happy lives. In John 9, we read that He sent a blind man to the pool. His obedience resulted in the restoration of his sight. In John 11, Mary and Martha rolled away the stone, and Lazarus lived. Those who do not obey His guidance miss the joy they could receive. What will you do with Jesus?

Nothing Secret—Nothing Cheap

Joshua 7:20-26

Introduction

    A. The story of Achan is one of the saddest stories in the Bible. Read Josh. 7:20-26. He was a member of the "church" but was playing games with God.

    B. Our scripture emphasizes three great truths for us to consider.

        1. Truth One: Sin cannot be hidden from God.

        2. Truth Two: Sin will be punished by God.

        3. Truth Three: The results of sin cannot be isolated.

    C. Review the story concerning Achan.

        1. Joshua was leading the children of Israel in the conquest of Canaan. God had promised to give Jericho to them but ordered that they would take no spoils of war (Josh. 6:18). God kept His promise, and Jericho was captured.

        2. Israel sinned and disobeyed God (Josh. 7:1). When Israel continued their conquest of the land, they were without the promise and suffered defeat (Josh. 7:2-5). Joshua was disturbed at the defeat and went before God to find out what was wrong (Josh. 7:6).

        3. God explained the problem, their failure, and the solution (Josh. 7:10-13).

    D. The consequences of disobedience have not changed today.

I. Lesson No. 1: Sin Cannot Be Hidden

    A. Achan's own account shows how careful he was (Josh. 7:21).

        1. No one was aware of his disobedience.

        2. God knew, and that was enough.

    B. Today, many people are following Achan's example.

        1. Teens do things behind their parents' backs, but God sees them.

        2. Adults cover up things, but God sees them.

      3. Illustrations could be multiplied about how sins rise to the surface of life.

  C. Sins will always be found out (Numb. 32:23). Illustration: David's sin with Bathsheba is a classic example.

II. Lesson No. 2: Sin Will Be Punished by God

  A. Examine Achan's sin. Ordinarily, the soldiers took the spoils of conquered enemies. However, God changed the rules and forbade it (Josh. 6:19).

  B. God has never smiled at sin, and He will not tolerate it today.

  C. We cannot change God's attitude by softening our response to sin.

      1. God hates sin because He is "a jealous God" (Exod. 20:5).

      2. God loves the sinner but hates sin and will always punish sinful actions.

III. Lesson No. 3: The Results of Sin Cannot Be Isolated

  A. Achan's sin caused suffering for many people.

      1. The whole nation of Israel suffered in defeat at Ai.

      2. Achan's entire family suffered because of his sin (v. 24).

      3. The cost of Achan's personal indulgence was extremely high.

  B. The price of sin cannot be isolated today.

      1. We have the freedom to do whatever we choose, but the costs involve others.

      2. We are intertwined social creatures, and our lives will affect others.

      3. Sinful acts can become a jungle of entanglement in the lives of many.

      4. Illustrate with a story of someone whose sins affected innocent people.

Conclusion

  A. Sin can be committed in secret but will someday come into the world's spotlight.

  B. Sin may cost nothing now, but the interest is building up and will be collected.

  C. Jesus invites you to deal with your sin today and save future anguish and agony of exposure and expense.

D. Will you respond to His invitation to forgive your sins and blot out the consequences today?

Jesus Passes By

Luke 18:35-43

Introduction

    A. When Jesus walked on earth, He made many dramatic changes. Because He passed through our world everything is dated from His birthday. Because He passed through our world it can be a better place for everyone.

    B. The effect of Jesus' coming can be seen in the lives of those whom He helped. To give us a foundation for our exploration, we will read from Luke 18:35-43. We will need to keep in mind that whatever Jesus did for anyone during Bible days He can still do for us today.

I. Because Jesus Passed By, a Blind Beggar Received His Sight

    A. This man had been unable to enjoy the things sighted people take for granted.

        1. He could not behold the beauty of the world in which he lived.

        2. He struggled to maintain the necessities of life.

        3. No one in his world could help him.

    B. When Jesus came his way, wonderful things happened.

        1. The Answer to his need was passing by.

        2. Some people tried to rebuke him and discourage him (v. 39).

        3. His determination was honored by the Master (vv. 40-43).

    C. Today, many people are blind to life's greater values.

        1. Jesus passes by and will make a difference if we will let Him.

        2. Some people may try to discourage you from believing.

        3. Jesus will change your life if you will trust Him.

II. Because Jesus Passed By a Widow's Sorrow Was Turned to Joy (Luke 7:11-16)

A. A widow had lost her only son and was left alone in the world.
   1. To be a widow in that day was a tragedy.
   2. It was a son's responsibility to provide for his mother.
   3. When he died, she had become helpless and without hope.

B. Jesus passed by as she was on her way to the cemetery.
   1. He was moved with compassion when He saw her need (v. 13).
   2. He gained her attention and changed her life (vv. 14-15).

C. Jesus is passing by our world today.
   1. He will do for us what no one else is able to do.
   2. He has compassion for us in our times of serious need and sorrow.

III. Because Jesus Passed By, a Stormy Night Became Calm (Mark 6:45-52)

A. The disciples were caught in a dreadful situation.
   1. Their obedience caused them to be in a perilous situation (v. 1).
   2. Even though Jesus was weary from the day's events, He knew where they were and went to help them.

B. Jesus passed by and met them at their point of need (v. 48).

C. Many people get caught in life situations that destroy them. But Jesus passes by and brings deliverance. Let Him into your boat (heart), and He will bring peace to you.

IV. Because Jesus Passed By, Sinners Were Forgiven (John 4:6)

A. This transformation took place in the lives of many.
   1. Look at: Matt. 9:9 (tax collector). Look at Luke 19:5 (Zacchaeus). Look at John 4:6 (the woman at the well).
   2. Each life was changed by Jesus' presence.

B. Jesus still changes lives today. All that He has ever done, He still desires to do.

Conclusion

A. In the scripture, when Jesus of Nazareth passed by wonderful things happened to obedient people.

B. Jesus of Nazareth is passing by right now and will make a marvelous change in the lives of all who will be obedient to Him. Illustration: Chuck Colson, one of the Watergate conspirators, was serving time in prison for his crime until Jesus of Nazareth passed by. He responded to Jesus' invitation, and his life was changed forever. Now he is being used to help multitudes to know Jesus.

C. Will you listen to Him so that He can change your life today?

Four Views from the Cross

Luke 23 and John 19

Introduction

A. Passover was a busy time in Jerusalem. Every Jew wanted to go to Jerusalem for the Feast of the Passover. The situation was so volatile that the ruling Romans reinforced the guard.

B. With a crowd that large it is only reasonable to assume that there was a mass of people on Calvary's hillside for the Crucifixion. They were like any group of people. They migrated to the action spot. Something critical to humankind was taking place on that hill outside the gate.

C. Jesus had gone through the mockery of a trial.

D. The shameful procession to the place of execution revealed the raw nature of people's lives that had not been tempered by God's love.

E. Jesus had been crucified and was hanging on the Cross waiting for death. The physical pain Jesus experienced was excruciating. In the worst physical situation possible, Jesus did not think of himself but others.

I. He Looked and Saw Misguided People (Luke 23:34)

A. The crowd gathered there was under the influence of powerful men.
   1. They had been taught to trust the Sanhedrin in such matters.
   2. The Sanhedrin had yielded to the influence of several powerful men.
   3. They had set events in motion that moved so rapidly the people were misguided.

B. Jesus still loved them and wanted them to experience forgiveness. He took the initiative to forgive those misled people (v. 34).

C. Jesus looks at us today with a desire that we will know forgiveness.

II. **Jesus Saw an Individual Who Wanted to Go to Heaven (Luke 23:39)**
  A. Who would have blamed Jesus if He had responded, "I can't be bothered. I have enough problems of my own."
    1. Jesus did not think of himself. He thought of others.
    2. Jesus had come to atone for people who had broken the commandments.
  B. This man was honest enough to admit his need.
    1. Note the difference in the men.
    2. The one who repented was forgiven. The one that was haughty died in his sin.

III. **Jesus Looked and Saw Two People Needing Special Attention (John 19:25-27)**
  A. Jesus saw the broken heart of His mother.
    1. He knew how much she loved Him.
    2. He also knew that it was the oldest child's responsibility to care for her.
    3. He instructed her to look to John for her needs.
  B. Jesus saw His brokenhearted friend, John.
    1. John was the one who felt Jesus' love very strongly.
    2. Jesus knew that John needed a way to demonstrate his love (see v. 27).
    3. Even in His hour of pain, Jesus helped others.
  C. What an amazing Savior He is! How encouraging it is to belong to Jesus who is so concerned about others that He disregarded His own physical suffering.

IV. **Jesus Looked Across the Pages of Time and Saw You and Me**
  A. Jesus was not only concerned about the crowd around the Cross. He was concerned about you and me.
  B. Jesus knew everything there was to know. Still He loved us (see Rom. 5:8).
    1. He is telling us that He does not condemn us. We are forgiven.
    2. He is telling us that sometimes we are misguided but He still loves us.
    3. He is saying that He will not leave us to struggle alone in the world.

Conclusion

   A. When Jesus was on the Cross, we were on His mind.
   B. Today, we stand at the foot of the Cross. If you listen,
      you will hear Him whisper, "I care enough to do this for
      you."
   C. Will you respond to His love for you?

The Great Homecoming

Revelation 7:9-17

Introduction

A. Homecomings and family reunions are great experiences. They are times when we see our friend and loved ones from the past. They are times of fellowship, smiles, and much happiness.

B. There is a homecoming for the family of God that is beyond our imagination.
1. Read the scripture: Rev. 7:9-17.
2. This is heaven—the eternal place where all of the family will come together. Just think of meeting our heroes of the faith from the Bible and church history.

C. That homecoming will be a time of great celebration. According to verses 10-12 there will be a lot of singing. There will be time to visit and enjoy each other. There will be a great meal—the Marriage Supper of the Lamb (Rev. 19:9).

I. Look at the Reality of Heaven

A. Heaven is not a figment of someone's imagination.
1. It is not understood by minds of humankind because of our limitations.
2. Our lack of understanding has nothing to do with this reality. It is our hope.

B. Heaven is taught clearly in the Bible.
1. Scripture contains 531 references to heaven.
2. Jesus spoke clearly about it in Matt. 6, John 14, and so forth.
3. Paul spoke of heaven (1 Cor. 15; 1 Thess. 4).
4. Peter spoke of heaven in 1 Pet. 1.

C. Most of the world believes in heaven.
1. There is an inherent belief in a better life by people who do not know Jesus.
2. This universal belief cannot be explained away by skeptics' denials.

II. Look at the Road to Heaven

A. It would be unfair to discuss heaven's reality without explaining how to get there.
1. In Matt. 5:8 Jesus said that heaven would be populated by purehearted people.
2. We get pure hearts when we confess our sins (1 John 1:9).
3. Paul writes in Rom. 10:9 how to be prepared.

B. The family reunion in heaven is being planned for very special people.
1. Only those who belong to the family of God will be invited. Illustration: Have you ever been invited to the family reunion of strangers?
2. The dress for that day is clearly defined in verse 9.
3. Activities for the day are spelled out in verses 9-10.
4. This clearly symbolizes that they are happy, joyful people. Unhappy people would be even more miserable in heaven.

C. How do we meet the conditions to qualify for being part of God's family? We begin at the foot of the Cross (v. 14).

D. The road to heaven comes from all over the world (v. 9). The journey to heaven is a route of praise (v. 12).

III. Look at the Results of Arriving at the Reunion

A. Will this reunion be worth the trip?
1. We will be released from the bondage of the flesh (v. 16).
2. Note Paul's statements in 1 Cor. 15:42-44.
3. See Paul's promise in Phil. 3:21. Illustrate with the story of a handicapped person who will be whole in heaven, such as Fanny Crosby and Helen Keller.

B. We will be released from all anxiety (v. 17 and Rev. 21:4).

C. Most of all it is an unending relationship with our Heavenly Father (v. 15).

Conclusion

A. This is one homecoming that I want to be sure to attend.

B. I hope that you will join me for that great celebration that Jesus is preparing.

C. He invites you to the family reunion.
D. Will you come?